# VRIL

OR

# VITAL MAGNETISM

SECRET DOCTRINE OF
ANCIENT ATLANTIS, EGYPT, CHALDEA
AND GREECE

## THE BOOK TREE
### ESCONDIDO, CALIFORNIA

# Vril, or Vital Magnetism

ISBN 978-1-58509-506-3

ORIGINALLY PUBLISHED 1911
BY A. C. McCLURG & CO.

Republished 1999 by
**The Book Tree
Post Office Box 724
Escondido, CA 92033**

# CONTENTS

This book is one of a series known as

# The Arcane Teaching

Reference is made herein, in several places, to
the other volumes of the series. Each volume
is complete in itself, and yet has a general relation to the others. The six volumes of the
series constitute a complete, though condensed,
library of the best esoteric and occult teachings
of the past, explained in modern terms and
adapted to the requirements of the present time.

# VRIL, OR VITAL MAGNETISM

## Introduction

Vril is another name for the life energy of the body, known in other cultures worldwide as mana, prana, chi, or vital force. Most of the ancient cultures of the world were aware of this important force and worked to make use of it.

In today's world, especially in the West, we move along through life completely oblivious to this truly vital force. Although this force cannot be seen, it is the life force within our bodies. It takes energy from food and provides muscles with energy, which in turn allows us to move about in daily life as well as grow and metabolize. Nourishment, digestion, and elimination are all driven by the life force.

Vril also has a connection to the mind, and methods can be employed to store up its energy and use it constructively. Vril is not manufactured in the human body, but can be collected and used effectively. This energy is present in water, and especially in the air. This is why breathing is so important in the practice of meditation. A deeper part of us comes alive while we meditate, due to increased vital energy in the body combined with the relaxation of the mind.

This book is by far the best guidebook known to this mysterious and powerful force. The exact mechanics of how it works are detailed, plus methods of gathering, conserving, and using its power. The exercises given are powerful and they work. This is really more of a self-help book than a simple fact book or mystical overview. Few books have packed in so much vital information in so few pages, and out of all the books we have ever seen, we can safely say that no other book from the West reveals anything close to the important information found here on this subject.

Paul Tice

# Vril, or Vital Magnetism

### LESSON I

#### THE NATURE OF VRIL

IN the Arcane Teaching, the term "Vril" indicates the universal principle of vital-energy, life-force, or vital magnetism, as it is sometimes called. The term itself is believed to have had its origin in the language of ancient Atlantis, tradition holding that the Atlantean root *vri*, meaning life, is the source of the word Vril, the latter expressing the idea of the vital principle or life-energy. This original root term is believed to have influenced similar elementary terms in the Sanscrit, and through this that great source of tongues, the Latin, from which our own language is largely derived. In many languages we find words indicating manly vigor, energy, virility, which undoubtedly owe their origin to the original Atlantean root term *vri* from which our term is derived.

In the ancient Greek we find the term *veros*,

meaning " a hero." In the Sanscrit we dis-
cover *vira,* meaning " a hero," and in the ancient Irish *vear,* meaning " a man." The
Gothic *wair,* and the Anglo-Saxon *wer,* each
meaning " a man," as well as the Latin word
*vir,* meaning " a man," (from which our terms
" virile, virility," originated,) also appear to
have been derived from the Atlantean term *vri,*
or " life." It was very natural to identify the
concept of " man " with " life." In our own
language the terms " virile " and " virility "
indicate life-force or vital-energy, particularly
in the sense of procreative power, the usage of
these terms bearing out the above stated theory
of their origin. Bulwer, who was well-versed
in occult tradition and terms, used the term
" vril " in one of his novels, to indicate a mysterious form of energy employed by a newly
discovered and highly advanced race of people, upon whose doings his story was based. It
is almost certain that Bulwer borrowed this
term from some of the ancient occult writings,
with which he was so familiar, and that the
ancient Arcane term " vril " was known to him.

In many of these ancient occult treatises we
find frequent reference to " Vril," not only in
its sense of the principle of vital energy, but

also in that sense of inherent usable energy
which we seek to express by the term "human
magnetism." In such writings we find the
term employed to explain many of the phenomena of occultism. Nearly, if not all, of the
schools of occultism, in all lands and in all
times, have taught the existence of this wonderful principle of energy. In Persian mys-
ticism the term *glama* is used in the same
sense; in Hindu occultism we find the word
*prana* serving a similar purpose. Mesmer
seems to have stumbled upon this truth when
he taught the existence of "the universal
fluid," although he was far from the truth in
his deductions therefrom. In the revival of
interest in occult science in western lands, so
noticeable in the past generation, and which
continues to the present time, we find frequent
references to "human magnetism," "animal
magnetism," "vital magnetism." And in the
schools of "magnetic healing" which attracted
so much attention about ten years ago, we
heard much of "the magnetic fluid." The existence of the principle of Nature which we call
"Vril" in the Arcane Teaching, has been recognized by many schools of thought throughout human history. Many names have been

given to it, and many theories have been advanced to account for its existence, and to explain its purposes and effects. We shall not attempt to go into the history of this idea, nor to consider the many attempted explanations above referred to. We prefer to go to the fountain head, and present the original Arcane Teaching regarding the principle of Vril.

In the Arcane Teaching, then, the term " Vril " is used in several senses, general and particular, as we shall see as we proceed. In the first place, Vril is held to be a great cosmic principle of very fine energy permeating all forms of matter, and immanent in thought processes as well, being employed by the principle of mind in its work of thinking. But Vril is not identical with mind. Mind is held to be a prior manifestation of the Infinite. From the mental principle arose Vril and the grosser forms of energy, and then the forms of matter fine and gross. In this original sense Vril is perceived to be a great universal principle from which proceeds a multitudinous manifestation of activities. Vril, in this phase of existence, cannot be defined any more than any universal principle can be defined. We have no words with which to define or explain it. It is only when we descend to the consideration of its manifestations that we are able to explain or define it in our finite terms.

In the second sense of the term, Vril is the principle of inner vital power or energy found to be immanent in all forms of specialized matter, inorganic or organic. It is this recognition of universal immanence that has led science to advance the new theories that Life is present in all forms of matter, even in the crudest and grossest states, phases and forms of matter. Haeckel boldly asserts that the atoms of matter possess something akin to life, and manifest the capability of perceiving something like sensations, *and the ability to respond thereto.* Haeckel says: "The two fundamental forms of substance, ponderable matter and ether, are not dead and only moved about by extrinsic force, but they are endowed with sensation and will (though naturally of the lowest grade); they experience an inclination for condensation, a dislike for strain; they strive after the one and struggle against the other."

Haeckel also says: "The different relations of the various elements toward each other, which chemistry calls 'affinity,' is one of the most important properties of ponderable matter; it is manifested in the different relative quantities or proportions of ponderable matter; it is manifested in the different relative quantities or proportions of their combination in the intensity of its consummation. Every shade of inclination, from complete indifference to the fiercest passion, is exemplified in the chemical action of the various elements toward each other, just as we find in the psychology of man, and especially in the life of the sexes. Goethe, in his classical romance, 'Affinities,' compared the relation of a pair of lovers with the phenomenon of the same name in the formation of chemical combinations. The irresistible passion that draws Edward to the sympathetic Ottilia, or Paris to Helen, and leaps over all bounds of reason and morality, is the same 'unconscious' attractive force which impels the living spermatozoon to force an entrance into the ovum in the fertilization of the egg of the animal or plant—the same impetuous movement which unites two atoms of hydrogen to one atom of oxygen for the formation of a molecule of water. This fundamental unity of affinity in the whole of nature, from the simplest chemical process to the most complicated love story, was recognized

by the Greek scientist, Empedocles, in the fifth
century B. C., in his theory of 'the love and
hate of the elements.' It receives empirical
affirmation from the interesting progress of
cellular psychology, the great significance of
which we have learned to appreciate in the last
thirty years. On those phenomena we base
our conviction that even the *atom* is not without a rudimentary form of sensation and will,
or, as it is better expressed, of feeling (*aesthe-
sis*) and inclination (*tropesis*)—that is, a universal 'soul' of the simplest character. The
same must be said of the molecules which are
composed of two or more atoms. Further
combinations of different kinds of these molecules give rise to simple and, subsequently,
complex chemical compounds, in the activity
of which the same phenomena are repeated in
a more complicated form."

Science now admits, nay, positively affirms,
that the principle of Life is immanent in, and
manifest through, all forms of material things,
inorganic as well as organic. We are not now
concerned with the idea of the presence of
mind in all of these forms, except inasmuch as
mind is always an accompaniment of life. Life
is generally defined as the quality of sensation

and will manifested in forms of matter. But a closer definition is now being advanced by science. The latest conception is that *Life consists in the power of independent action and movement*—that is, in the ability to act and move from inner and inherent power, and not from power or force applied from without. It is this very *power* to act and move which the Arcane Teaching holds to be the second phase of the existence of Vril. A body may possess sensation and will — ability to feel, and ability to exercise volition — and yet not be able to act and move. Feeling and will are mental states or qualities — but the power which acts and moves is something different from mind, for it is what is called vital-force, life-energy, or Vril. A man may *feel* the sting of an insect, and may then *will* to brush aside the insect. But unless (by the exercise of his will, usually, but sometimes by reflex activity) he sends a current of vital-force, life-energy, nervous energy — Vril, in short — his muscles will not contract nor will his hand move. Moreover, without Vril he cannot even perform the processes of thought, and come to a decision regarding the brushing away of the insect. *Vril is the force which operates the machinery of life from the crudest movement up to the highest exercise of the brain cells of the philosopher or mathematician.*

Vril, then, in its second phase of manifestation or existence, is the inner power of action and movement of all material forms of the universe. It is by the action of Vril that the *ions*, electrons, corpuscles, or particles of elementary matter are attracted and repelled, and by which they engage in the wild whirl around each other which resembles the movement of the planets around our sun, which attraction and repulsion and consequent "whirl" combine to form what we know as the *atom* of matter. Likewise, it is Vril which causes these atoms to be attracted and repelled, and to manifest constant vibration, thereby forming the combinations which give to us our eighty elements of matter. And it is by Vril that the molecules (formed of two or more atoms) manifest their varying degrees of cohesion and other molecular qualities, properties, and attributes, and thus give us the distinctive qualities of matter in all of its various forms. Vril, then, is the fine energy of force which enables material things to move of their own power — *the power within them.* Vril *is*, in itself, this *power within,* which enables the particle or atom of matter to move to and fro; which enables the atoms to form their combinations; which causes the molecules to manifest their qualities; which enables man to bend his arm and direct his pen at the behest and command of his will, urged thereto by his feelings or desires, and supervised by his intellectual reasoning.

Moreover, Vril is at the heart of the great mystery of science — Gravitation; that force which operates over infinities of space without the measure of time, and in spite of obstacles and interferences. Gravitation, which contradicts all the minor laws of physics, is seen really to be Vril, life-energy, and vital-force, in its second phase of manifestation. Vril, in the second phase of manifestation, pervades all space — it is immanent in the universal ether. Wherever *anything* is, *Vril* is, in its second phase of manifestation. The above is quite inadequate to give a complete idea of the existence and nature of Vril, but it is sufficient for our purposes at this time.

# LESSON II

## VRIL IN ORGANIC LIFE

VRIL, in the third sense of the term, or the third phase of its manifestation or existence, is the life-force or vital-energy of all organic forms of life—of all living creatures. From the single cell or moneron in the slime of the ocean-bed, or the lowly quasi-organic forms of green sediment or deposits on rocks and old trees, to the highest forms of animal and human life, Vril is ever present and operative. Just as protoplasm is the peculiar phase of matter which serves as the body of living organisms, so is this phase or form of Vril the peculiar force or energy which always accompanies organic life. In fact it is the distinctive property or attribute of organic life. When science is forced to decide whether or not a thing is "living" in the ordinary sense of the term, it is the possession or non-possession of this form of Vril which serves to decide the matter and make the distinction. It is this third phase of manifestation of Vril which forms the subject matter of our present consideration in this book.

Vril, in its third phase of manifestation, is the energy which performs the functions of life in the living organism. It is the power by which the living creature carries on the processes of digestion, assimilation, excretion, nourishment, repair, and elimination. It is the power by which it moves its body by conscious will, and by which the subconscious movements of the cells and organs of the body are performed. Vril causes the heart to beat, and the arteries and veins to carry and propel the blood in its outward and inward course. It causes the intestines and other canals to manifest their peculiar peristaltic action. It is the power by which the will moves the hand and fingers, and by means of which these words are written. We are accustomed to thinking that the *will* causes these movements, and so it does, but only indirectly. The will is a mental phase; it chooses to make the movement, after which it releases or projects the Vril along the channels of the nerves to the muscles. The muscles then contract, and the movement is effected. The will is like the operator managing one of the great cranes in a modern steel

works, who touching a button here, and a lever
there, swings the mighty instrument in any
direction, causing it to descend upon a great
mass of steel, lift it up, and swing it to any
desired point. But the man and the machinery
could never cause the crane to do this work if
there was not available the *power* (electricity
or steam) subject to the control and direction
of the operator. Vril in the human body is
like electricity in the trolley car—it is *that
which makes things " go."*

While Vril is distributed all over the human
body—even the tiniest cell having its share—
it is found principally in the two great nervous systems, and is stored up in the great
reservoirs of the brain, the spinal-cord, and
the various plexi or ganglia of the nervous system. For the purposes of simple conception
and easy thinking, we may regard this phase
of Vril as the "nervous fluid," or nerve-force,
of physiology, remembering always, however,
that it is no more a "fluid" than is magnetism
or electricity, and that it is not a mechanical
force. It is much nearer to mind-power than
it is to ordinary physical force, and yet it is
different from either. Its place is between
mind-power and physical force, while some-

what resembling both.  All attempts to identify Vril with mind-power or physical force
must fail, for it is a thing of itself — a distinct
manifestation of nature or that which lies behind nature.

There is manifested in some quarters a dis-
position to consider " vital force " or " vitality " as a distinct entity or " soul " which energizes the physical body, and the same dispo-
sition may be manifested by students in their
consideration of the third phase of Vril.  This
is an error, and all the best authorities positively condemn it as such.  For instance, Hux-
ley, in speaking of the principle of " vitality,"
says:  " Considered apart from the phenomena
of consciousness, the phenomena of life are all
dependent upon the working of the same physical and chemical forces as those which are active in the rest of the world.  It may be conv6n-
ient to use the terms ' vitality,' and ' vital
force ' to denote the causes of certain great
groups of natural operations, as we employ the
names of ' electricity ' and ' electrical force ' to
denote others, but it ceases to be proper to do
so if such a name implies the absurd assump-
tion that either ' electricity ' or ' vitality ' are

*entities* playing the part of efficient causes of electrical or vital phenomena."

In the same way, it is erroneous to consider Vril as an *entity* or soul, directly and immediately causing the activities and movements of the body. Vril is not the soul, spirit, or mind, of the person any more than it is his physical body, but is a mighty natural force operating upon the body under the control of the conscious or subconscious mental faculties. Its activities manifest in and by means of the physical bodily forms and structure, it is true, but they are inspired and directed by the mind, conscious or subconscious. The physical form may and does *carry* its charge of Vril, but does not *produce* the latter. Vril *energizes and moves* the physical structure, but does not *cause* it. In a similar manner, while Vril is active in every process of thought, it is not produced by thought; and while it energizes thought processes, it does not *produce* thought in the sense of *causing* it. Mind (in the ordinary sense); Vril, either as a principle or in its manifestation; and Matter, either as a principle or in manifestation; are *the three co-ordinate manifested principles* of the Infinite, and depend upon each other for their activities.

This is the teaching not only of modern science, but also of the ancient Arcane sages.

In the previous volumes of this series devoted to the Arcane Teaching, we have seen that Matter exists in forms far more tenuous, subtle, and fine than any known to the senses of man; and also in forms far more gross than the imagination of man can picture. In the same teaching we may see that, even more subtle than the finest forms of matter mentioned, there exist etheric substances infinitely rare, tenuous and refined. The same is true regarding the teaching concerning Vril. Not only do we see Vril manifesting in the inner movements of the *ions,* atoms, and molecules of matter, and again in its finer phases of animal and human life, but the teaching is that there are forms and manifestations of Vril so much higher than the latter that the ordinary human mind would be unable to conceive of them. But the principle of Vril is ever the same, in high or low manifestation. Much that is called "psychic phenomena" is explainable only by a knowledge of the existence, principles and laws of Vril, as set forth in the Arcane Teachings. Even the ordinary processes of thought are performed by the aid of Vril in a manner not as yet understood by ordinary men, or even by the physical scientists. It remains for the occultist to state and understand the finer forces of nature, as manifest in the processes which we call "thought."

Many of us confuse the idea of "thought" with that of "mind," but the occultist and scientist know better than this. Mind, in itself, is a great principle the exact nature of which cannot be grasped by the ordinary mind. Thought, on the contrary, is a manifestation of mind, assisted by Vril. The material scientist who perceives the operation of Vril in the processes of thought, and who recognizes the relationship between these processes and that of the physical world, is right so far as he goes, for the activities of Vril are employed therein, just as they are in many physical and chemical processes for reasons which we have already stated. But he makes a wrong induction who holds that, by reason thereof, thought is merely "a secretion of matter," or "a by-product of matter." He fails to realize that Mind is the original cause of thought, and that it employs Vril in its thought processes just as it employs the fine matter of the brain-cells in these processes. It is only when we recog-

nize the co-existence and co-ordination of
Mind, Vril, and Matter, that we are able to
perceive the real underlying causes of the phenomena of thought.

Physical science is also in error when it attempts to limit the activities of "vital-force"
or "nerve-force" (which are but names for
the activities of one phase of Vril) to the particular human body in which it is generated or
stored. Science loses the opportunity to satis-
factorily account for much perplexing phenomena, by insisting upon this antiquated and
narrow conception. That which is generally
termed "psychic phenomena" is explainable
only when the fact of the "long-distance"
effect of Vril is perceived and admitted. Likewise, many of the metaphysicians and pseudo-
occultists are in error when they attempt to
account for certain psychic phenomena by the
hypothesis of "mind action" alone. *The mind
cannot produce effect at a distance without the
employment of the power of Vril,* any more
than the wireless-telegraph operator can produce his long-distance effects by his own will
unaided by the power employed in his wonderful instruments.

The physiologist who leaves Vril out of his

calculations is no more at sea than is the modern metaphysician or "mental scientist" who omits it from his theories, explanations, and experiments. Without the power of Vril there could be none of the phenomena of mentalism, made so popular by the new schools of mental science and the great revival of interest in ancient occultism which has distinguished the present generation. The mental scientist who understands the nature and methods of employment of Vril, is enabled to double his successes. He uses Vril, of course, unconsciously and unknowingly, in all of his experiments and work — but he wastes more energy than he uses. It is only when he understands the nature of Vril, and the methods of its employment in his mental science work, that he can hope to project his mental power effectively and efficiently. Yet so carried away with their metaphysical theories are some of these practitioners, that they iterate and reiterate "all is mind," and deny even the existence of such a principle as Vril.

Those who assert that "thoughts are things" are right so far as they go — but they do not go far enough. A thought cannot be generated without Vril. Neither can it be projected to a distance without a peculiar employment of the force of Vril. The earnest belief and active faith of many practitioners of mental science causes them to unconsciously energize their thought with Vril, in spite of their denials of its existence. If they would lay aside some of their prejudices, and investigate the subject of Vril, they could and would be enabled so to energize their thought that their power and success would be redoubled. The narrow metaphysician is as much in error as is the narrow materialist. It is only when *the triangle of being* — Mind, Vril, and Matter — is recognized, that one's full powers and energies may be manifested.

# LESSON III

## THE MECHANISM OF VRIL

THE student should bear in mind that Vril is never *manufactured* in the human body There is just so much Vril in existence — a certain amount or quantity — and this amount or quantity never can be added to, nor subtracted from, by the organism of man. Just as the instruments employed in electrical science gather up, store up, and transform into various forms and phases the electricity already in existence in nature, without creating or destroying a single particle thereof, so does the organism of man gather from the principle of Vril that which it requires; so does it store up a reserve supply of Vril; so does it transform Vril into the various forms and phases required for the purposes of the organism; and so does it use Vril in its activities. But the Vril so gathered, stored, and transformed is never created by the organism; nor is the Vril so used ever destroyed. The seeming creation is merely the absorption of the Vril needed, from the uni-

27

versal supply thereof; and the seeming destruction is merely the return of Vril to the universal supply thereof. Vril is never created nor destroyed — it merely undergoes transformation of phase, form, and use.

The mechanism of the human body involved in the absorption, storage, transformation, and use of Vril, is that which is known in ordinary physiology as "the nervous system." Very few persons know the facts concerning this most wonderful mechanism of the human organism, which is employed as the mechanism of the activities of Vril. In order to understand the activities of Vril, the student should have at least an elementary knowledge of the human nervous system. Accordingly, we invite you to a brief consideration thereof.

The nervous system of the human being is divided into two great systems, *viz.*, the cerebro-spinal system and the sympathetic system. The cerebro-spinal nervous system consists of that part of the general nervous system which is composed of the brain and the spinal cord, together with the nerves which emerge from the latter. Its functions are those connected with the processes of sensation, volition, and the higher processes of thought. It conveys to the brain the reports of the organs of feeling, seeing, smelling, hearing, and tasting. It manifests consciousness and the phenomena thereof. It attends to the functions of thought. It is the channel and mechanism of action. Through it the individual receives knowledge of the outside world, and communicates information to the outside world. It has been compared to a telegraph system, the brain being the great central station, the spinal column being the cable running from the central office, and the nerves being the connecting telegraph wires running to the minor stations of the body.

The brain of man consists of three parts, known, respectively, as the medulla oblongata, the cerebellum, and the cerebrum. The medulla oblongata is situated at the upper end of the spinal cord, and is an enlargement of the upper portion thereof. It is a reflex centre of a high order. It controls, to a certain extent, certain functions of the sympathetic nervous system, and therefore the activities of the heart, lungs, blood-vessels, and the abdominal organs. Its activities are out of the ordinary field of consciousness, and belong to those of the subconscious mind. The cerebellum, sometimes known as "the little brain," lies just above the medulla oblongata, and like it is a reflex centre of a high order. Its purpose is to co-ordinate the muscular movements of the body, and to function along the line of acquired reflexes.

When we have learned to perform certain regular muscular movements so that they become habitual, we have really passed their execution on to the cerebellum. As we all know, when we first learn to perform a new and difficult task, such as walking, riding, skating, writing, or running a machine, we must pay conscious attention to it, the cerebrum being the part of the brain then employed. But when we have mastered the rudimentary motions so that they may be performed with very little conscious attention, the cerebellum takes charge, and the actions are thereafter performed almost automatically and unconsciously by reason thereof. In habitual muscular activity the cerebrum merely initiates the motion, and then the cerebellum takes it up and continues it subconsciously. When the cerebellum is injured, the gait is affected and the individual often loses the power to perform many of the usual reflex actions.

Professor Halleck says of the importance of the reflex activities mentioned: " Thus the mind is not only saved the trouble of attending to every little movement, but much time is gained. After the child has learned the difficult art of balancing himself on his feet, walking becomes largely a reflex act. At first the child must centre his whole attention on movements to balance the body. The man can think out the most complex problems while walking, because the reflex nervous centres are superintending the balancing process. Few men remember which end of the collar they button on first, or which shoe they put on first; yet the reflex nerve centre, if left to itself, has an invariable order in executing these movements." Professor Gordy says: " The cerebellum is the organ for many acquired reflexes . . . All that seems necessary for the mind or consciousness to have to do with it is to set the machine well going, so to speak, when some part of the nervous mechanism relieves consciousness of all further work in the matter."

The cerebrum, or "large brain" occupies the greater part of the entire cavity of the skull. It is the headquarters of consciousness, to which the nerves of sensation report. A blow that affects the cerebrum produces unconscious-

ness.  The nervous connection with the cerebrum must be maintained, else the sensation is
not felt.  An injury to the cerebrum impairs
the faculties of thought and of memory.  From
this and other reasons, science knows that the
cerebrum is the part of the brain most closely
related to consciousness and intelligence.  But
its quality and functions vary materially in its
various parts.  The "cortex," or thin rind or
outer covering of gray matter, is held to be
the seat of intellectual activity and consciousness.  Moreover, there exists in the cerebrum,
what is known as "localization of functions,"
that is to say that certain parts or areas of the
cerebrum are devoted to special functional activity.  For  instance,  there  is  the  "motor
zone," from which are sent out the orders to
transmit Vril so as to move any part of the
body.  Science has so definitely located these
zones that "it is possible for a surgeon to find
the small centre which moves the vocal cords,
directs a thumb, or winks an eye."  Then there
are the "sensory tracts," which receive impres-
sions from the senses.  The various sense centres have been located with a surprising degree
of accuracy.  Science has not as yet succeeded
in localizing the intellectual areas definitely, al-

though phrenology has done something in that direction.

The spinal cord is continuous with the brain, the two forming parts of the same system. The spinal cord occupies the canal in the centre of the spinal column, or "backbone." It is composed of gray matter and white matter. It is almost separated into two parts by fissures, but there always remains a ridge of connecting nerve matter something like the connecting bar in the letter H. From the spinal cord emerge thirty-one pairs of spinal nerves, springing from either side of the cord, each nerve having two roots, an anterior and a posterior. An authority says of the functions of these nerves and roots: "If the foot were pricked, the sensory impulse would enter the spinal cord by the posterior root. The spinal ganglia would set free a motor impulse, which would leave for the foot by the anterior root of the nerve. If the posterior root of the nerve supply of the foot were cut, the foot might be crushed without a sensation of pain, but a motor impulse could be sent as before. If the anterior or motor root were cut, the application of a hot iron would cause as much pain as ever, but the sufferer could not move the foot an inch from the iron, no matter how great the pain.  A large part of the body is absolutely dependent upon the integrity of the spinal cord for the transmission of sensory and motor impulses.  If a person's back is broken, that part of the body supplied by nerves attached to the spinal cord below the seat of injury is paralyzed.  Such an unfortunate might watch the amputation of his own leg with as little feeling of pain as if the limb belonged to another person.  No act of will would suffice to move such a limb."

The above authority also says, regarding what is called " reflex action ": " Reflex nervous action is the result of that power resident in nervous ganglia, which often unconsciously causes many muscular and vital movements. The spinal cord is largely made up of such masses of nervous matter, which have sometimes been called ' little brains.'  If one were to prick the toe of a sleeper, the sensory nerve at that point would report the fact to one of the lower spinal nerve masses.  This ganglion, without waiting to hear from the brain, would issue a command to the motor nerve, and the foot would be immediately withdrawn.  Unless the thrust were severe, the sleeper would not awake, nor would he be conscious of pain or of the movement of his foot. This nervous action is called 'reflex,' because, when the sensory nerve conveys an impulse to the ganglion, this impulse is at once, and without the action of the will, reflected back by a motor nerve. Thus the mind is not only saved the trouble of attending to every little movement, but much time is gained."

The nerves emerging from the spinal column divide and subdivide and finally reach every part of the body. Like the wires of a great telegraph system they reach every point, important or insignificant. Without these nerves thus reaching every part of the body, some parts of the body would be without connection with the brain and would be cut off from the supply of Vril, or vital-energy. These nerves serve to convey sensation from a part to the brain, and to carry in return a motor or movement impulse and supply of Vril from the brain to the part. The nerves are classed as follows: (1) afferent nerves, which carry a stimulus from some part of the body to the central nervous system; and (2) efferent nerves, which transmit the motor impulse, or incentive to movement, from the central system to the part. The sensory nerves are afferent

nerves; the motor nerves are efferent nerves.
But there are other nerves of both afferent and
efferent classes, in addition to the sensory and
motor nerves just mentioned.   As an authority
says:   "In addition to these  .  .  .  there
are nerves which regulate the size of the blood
vessels and the nourishment of the body, control the secretions, and perform various other
offices connected with transmitting stimuli,
which are neither sensory nor motor."   The
nerve-cells are tiny knots of bunches of nerve
matter, connected with nerve fibres.   They are
of various shapes.   A *ganglion* (which, as we
have seen, performs reflex action) is a group,
confederation, or aggregation of nerve cells.
Each ganglion may be called a "little brain,"
for it resembles the brain in many respects.
The spinal ganglia receive sensory impulses
and in return send forth motor impulses to
action.

The second great division of the general
nervous system is that known as *the sympathetic nervous system*.   This great nervous system has control of the involuntary processes,
such as nutrition, growth, repair, elimination,
digestion, respiration, circulation.   It is situated principally in the thoracic, abdominal,

and pelvic cavities, and is distributed to the internal organs. It consists of a double-chain of ganglia on the sides of the spinal column, with scattered ganglia in the head, neck, chest and abdomen. These ganglia are connected with each other by filaments, and are also connected with the cerebro-spinal system by motor and sensory nerves. From the ganglia, numerous branches of fibres reach out to the various organs of the body, the blood-vessels, etc. At various points in the body, the sympathetic nerves meet and form nerve-masses called *plexi,* of which the solar plexus is the principal and largest one.

The solar plexus is a great mat of sympathetic nerves, situated in the epigastric region, on either side of the spinal column, immediately back of what is generally known as "the pit of the stomach." It is composed of both gray and white brain matter, similar to that which composes the brains of man, and is quite a complex centre. It plays an important part in the subconscious processes of the body, and is very sensitive — a blow over its region has been known to produce death, and in a celebrated prize-fight of some years ago it was the place to which the "knock-out blow" was directed. Its importance is being realized by science, more particularly during the past few years. By some authorities it has been called the "abdominal brain." It is the great store-house of that form of Vril which supplies the organs of the body which are concerned with nutrition, general vitality, the reproductive system, the circulation, and the nerves them-selves. Moreover, it serves as a reserve storage battery from which even the brain may draw power in times of necessity, and which, after effecting a slight transformation, it may use effectively.

It must be remembered that ordinarily the processes of the sympathetic nervous system are performed subconsciously and without call-ing on the conscious mind for aid or guidance. But the sympathetic nervous system may be and often is affected by the action of the con-scious mind acting upon it along the lines of "suggestion," and often causing it to perform its work improperly and poorly. In the same way, however, the conscious mind may suggest to the subconscious, and thus affect the sympa-thetic nervous system in the direction of helpful ideas and impulses. The conscious mind of the trained individual may reach any of the organs of his body, and not only may send them currents of Vril and thus strengthen and build them up, but by moving the involuntary muscles supporting them may even give them internal exercise. The man or woman who understands the art of suggesting to the subconscious mind, and of directing currents of Vril to the parts of the body, may keep his or her system in perfect condition and functioning power, and thus reach an old age of health, vigor, and virility.

By this method not only an additional nerve-stimulus may be given to every part of the body by means of both sets of nerves (cerebro-spinal and sympathetic) but the circulation of blood may also be so directed by the will, and when charged with Vril may invigorate any or all parts of the body, at will. All of these features of the use of Vril by means of the trained will, will be considered during our treatment of the subject in this book. At present our only purpose is to explain the mechanism in, by, over, and through which Vril operates in the human organism.

## LESSON IV

VRIL is in physical manifestation in every activity or function of the body. From the slightest movement of the cell to the more complex activities of the organs of the physical body, Vril is seen to be in manifestation and activity. The subconscious planes of the mind of the individual have control of the majority of the physical activities and functions, the conscious mind not being drawn into the activity. But in these subconscious processes Vril is ever the active force and power by means of which the work is performed. The subconscious mind without the power of Vril would be like a man without arms, hands, or tools, who would seek to perform skilled manual labor. On the other hand, Vril without the directing impulses of the subconscious mind would be like the arms, hands, and tools, apart from the directing power of the brain of the workman. It is by the power of Vril that the acorn grows into the oak, and the blade of grass forces its way through the hard soil. It is by the power of Vril that the single reproductive cell of the parents develops, grows, and evolves into the babe at birth, and later into the adult man or woman. There is, of course, always mind behind these activities, but there is also always Vril power to perform the work of that mind.

Science teaches us that the body is composed of a multitude of single cells, which forming in groups of greater or less size and degree of complexity, constitute the organs and parts of the body. Each tiny cell has its own degree of mentality, and each its own little charge of Vril. These cells are as tireless workers as the bees in a hive. There is constant activity in the realm of the cells. Day and night, without haste and without rest, these little cells are being born, are performing their life tasks, and are dying, being cast from the system and supplanted by new cells which have evolved from them. Every cell is, to an extent, an independent entity — an individual. But this individuality is often merged with that of other cells, and a co-operative cell-community is formed for the purpose of performing that portion of the common task of the socialistic commonwealth of the body.

Some of the cells are stationary, while others are operating under a roving commission. Some are on the scouting line, while others are engaged in actual warfare with the invaders of the body.   Others still are held as a reserve corps, awaiting a special call to action.   A great body of cells performs the work of the day-laborer, and does the drudgery of the community.   Others are engaged in the processes of thought, and are consumed by these activities, millions of cells giving up their lives to produce a single piece of continued thought-work.   Some of the cells perform the work of carriers, conveying new material in the blood to all parts of the body, where other cells build it up into physical form — the carrying cells are the hod-carriers and the brick-carriers of the system, while the building cells are like the bricklayers, carpenters, and other artisans.

Other cells are busily engaged in carrying away the debris, worn-out tissue and dead cells, to the great crematory of the lungs, where the waste matter is burned up by the oxygen and cast off through the exhaled breath.   Other cells perform the odd jobs of scavenger work, and carry the waste matter to other parts of the system, where it is cast off in excrementitious form. Other cells attend to the work of digestion, purification, assimilation; the chemical laboratories of the system being very extensive and complicated. Other cells are as living instruments and telegraph wires in the nervous system, and receive, send, and transmit the messages of the system, acting, as well, as transmitters of the additional supply of Vril required in various parts of the body. The standing army and police-force of the cell community are very large. These protectors and guardians of the body protect the system from the invading germs, bacteria, and other foreign organisms which have found entrance to it. They attack the invaders, and either devour them or else cast them forth from the system through the ordinary channels or by means of boils, pimples, and other eruptions.

The large force of cells employed in the great chemical laboratories of the system is kept very busy at all times. There is oxygen and food-substances to be used by cell-groups in all parts of the body. There is carbonic-acid refuse, and burnt up material to be cast off.

There is food to be converted into proper form
and condition to nourish the system. There is
gastric juice, saliva, pancreatic juices, bile,
milk, procreative fluids, to be manufactured
constantly. To give one an idea of the number
of cells so employed, the authorities have esti-
mated that in each single cubic inch of blood
there are at least 75,000,000 of the red blood
cells alone, not to speak of the white corpuscles and the other classes of cells. Seventy-
five million in one single cubic inch — think of
that! And each one of this army actuated by
mind, and carrying its tiny charge of Vril!
And we should remember that at every moment of our lives, from birth to death, the
great army of cells is constantly at work building, repairing, renovating, replacing, every
portion of our bodies. In a few weeks our
bodies are almost entirely made over. It requires an enormous amount of energy and
power to perform this work — and that power
is always Vril-power, for there is no other
power that can do the work, or by which the
work can be done. There is a constant using-
up of Vril-power, and there must needs be
a constant replenishing of the store of Vril in
the body.

In addition to the expenditure of Vril in the processes of the cells, we find that there is also an enormous expenditure in the voluntary activities of the individual. Each individual is like a great piece of machinery. He moves about, walks, runs, or leaps. He moves his arms and legs, his hands, his fingers, and his entire body, in the activities of waking-life. Every motion of the body, even the slightest, causes an expenditure of Vril-power, and each expenditure must be paid for by a decrease in the store of Vril in the system. Each item of expenditure must be counterbalanced by a renewal of the supply, else there is physical deterioration and loss of energy to the individual. Many persons are so prodigal of their Vril, and so ignorant or heedless regarding the renewal of the supply, that they become depleted in vitality, virility, and general nervous energy, and become physical wrecks or else subjects of the so-called neurasthenia or "nervous prostration" which so sorely afflicts the modern race. This result is not caused by excessive thinking, as so many suppose, for the brain will stand an immense amount of regular, arduous labor without manifesting evil results. It is the emotional excesses (emotion consuming an enormous amount of Vril), and the "waste-motion," which tends to this depletion.

Moreover, the average man or woman who suffers from nervous breakdown is not aware of the need of the system for calm repose and relaxation for the purpose of recharging the system with Vril. Even in sleep these persons keep their nervous system and muscles at a tension, and exhaust their supply of Vril just as the careless housewife exhausts the household supply of water by allowing the faucets to dribble and drip. The prevention of this waste of Vril is a very important matter, second only in importance to the knowledge of the proper methods of acquiring a more than ordinary supply of Vril in order to meet the requirements of modern life in a civilization which is seemingly bent upon burning up nerve-energy. The ordinary person, pursuing the even tenor of man's natural life, has very little need of instruction along these lines, for he neither wastes nor expends in work more Vril than is normally supplied to the system by means of the impulses of the subconscious mind. But the man of the large cities of to-day persistently wastes an abnormal amount of Vril, as well as expends in work an also unreasonable amount, and unless he makes up the deficit by the methods made known by a study of the subject, he will suffer by reason thereof.

It is deemed extremely probable, according to eminent thinkers along these lines, that in the course of the evolution of the race, nature will adapt the supply of Vril to the increased needs of the race, and the whole matter will adjust itself accordingly. But nature works as slowly as it works surely, and it will be some time before it feels the necessity of automatically adjusting the Vril conditions to meet the unnatural requirements and expenditures of modern life in our large centres of industry. Until then, man should help nature along, as he has in many other ways, and by preventing the unnatural waste, and increasing the supply of Vril by methods such as we shall describe in this book, he will be able to maintain an equilibrium and balance, with consequent preservation of health and energy. He may even go still further and by increasing his supply of Vril he may so charge himself with this life-energy and nerve-force as to become a very dynamo of energy, activity, and power. The man or woman doing this will possess a mighty advantage over the majority of the race at this time.   Such a course will mean increased efficiency, increased power, and increased success — and, let us hope, increased happiness.

# LESSON V

WE have seen that Vril, in its second phase, is inherent in all forms of atomic matter, and consequently in all forms of matter resulting from combinations of material atoms. As all matter is composed of material atoms, it follows then that Vril is to be found in *all* matter. But there is a vast difference in the forms and the conditions in and under which it so appears. Just as matter is the same whether appearing in the form and condition of the diamond or hardest steel, or in the form and condition of bread and butter, so in the same way it may be said that Vril is the same in principle whether it appears in the granite rock or in the air. But it is likewise true that just as steel and diamond cannot be used by man as a source of physical nourishment in the same way that bread and butter can be so used, so Vril in the granite rock is not available to man in the same way as is Vril in the air, the water, and in protoplasmic food material.

49

While all things in nature are, at the last, one in substance and principle, nevertheless the laboratory of nature forms many combinations and imposes many conditions upon these things, thereby fitting some things to one purpose and other things to other purposes. Here is where science steps in and insists upon the practical side of things as opposed to the " pure principles" of metaphysics. As an authority once said: " Those who like to study the puzzles as to what mind and matter really are, must go to metaphysics. Should we ever find that salt, arsenic, and all things else, are the same substance with a different molecular arrangement, we should still not use them interchangeably." And so to the man who may object that "Vril is Vril," we would remark that, while "matter is matter," he would do well to select protoplasmic forms of matter for food, rather than diamonds or steel — the same principle applying to Vril in its application to human requirements.

Nature has so wisely arranged matters that the supply of Vril, in its second phase, is found in its most usable form for man — in the precise combinations which meet the requirements of its transmutation into the third-phase condition, in which alone man may use it — in those very forms of substances which man employs in his physical economy for other purposes. Vril, in the precise combination required for transmutation for man's requirements, is found (1) in the protoplasmic substances which man naturally partakes of as food and nourishment; (2) in a lesser degree, in the water which man drinks in order to preserve his fluid-balance and to eliminate from his system the waste matter; and (3) in a high degree in the atmospheric air which man breathes into his lungs for the purpose of obtaining oxygen to serve in maintaining bodily heat, and to burn up the waste-matter of the system, both in the cell itself and in the lungs. Thus, we see, man may know nothing whatever regarding the principle and uses of Vril, and yet will be compelled by nature to partake of those very substances to which it inheres.

Under normal circumstances the individual will secure sufficient Vril by the "hit or miss" system of eating, drinking, and breathing practiced by him, without any particular instruction on the subject. But, as we have said, the unusual conditions in which modern man lives, particularly in the large cities, are such that

there is a greater waste and a greater use of
Vril than Nature has intended or provided for,
and, accordingly, the man who so dissipates
one of Nature's greatest forces must replace
and replenish it by extraordinary means. He
must bring his intellect to the aid of his subconscious mind, and supply that which in the
ordinary course of his life he may fail to secure. This is in no way contrary to nature.
It is merely aiding nature in her work. We
see instances of this in other features connected
with the physical well-being of man. For instance, man in the natural state does not need
to be urged to exercise, for his ordinary voca-
tion and day's work supplies him with all the
exercise he requires. But the man whose work
keeps him indoors and at the desk does not obtain the normal amount of exercise or out-of-
doors experience, and accordingly he is compelled to walk for his health and to practise
various forms of "artificial" exercise. The
natural man does not need to take a vacation
and indulge in fishing, boating, golfing, for his
physical well-being, while his brother in the
city is advised to do that for recreation which
the natural man does from necessity. The example of an eminent statesman felliing trees for

exercise and recreation, while the woodcutter finds nothing but "work" in the same employment, is another illustration of this fact.

So in this little book we shall have something to say regarding the means and methods whereby one who is deficient in Vril-force may obtain that which he needs and which he can not get in the ordinary way. The man leading the natural life in the woods and with sufficient physical exercise to bring into action the Vril-absorbing functions, will not need this instruction — it is not for him. But it is highly important that the average individual who reads this book should take advantage of the simple, natural, rational system and methods herein advanced. This ancient teaching is highly practicable and applicable to modern conditions. We may apply these teachings of a past civilization to the requirements of our own, with great benefit.

## LESSON VI

ORDINARY physiology does not recognize the element of Vril in food, but concerns itself with much important discussion of "calorics," "proteids," "food-units," all of which is very well and proper, for a scientific knowledge of food elements and the values thereof is important. In the state of nature man instinctively selects the class and variety of food best adapted for his needs. The centuries of human experience have built up an almost infallible instinct in this respect which man may safely follow under normal conditions. But so artificial are the conditions under which the majority of us live that instinct is almost stifled, and a most unnatural system of nourishment prevails. Accordingly, instruction upon this point is much needed by the race. But we have no intention of discussing this phase of the question of nourishment or food. The work has been well done by many others and the information concerning the same is at the call of nearly every person. Our purpose here is to consider food merely from the standpoint of its Vril-containing properties.

There is a vast difference in the amount and form of Vril in the various forms and kinds of foods. The foods rich in proteids contain much Vril in a form readily available to man. The carbohydrates are also charged with considerable Vril. The fats contain but little Vril in a form available for man — very little real energy, but much heat-producing material. But man in his unscientific methods of obtaining nourishment fails to secure either the best food-value or the greatest amount of Vril from any class of foods. Modern science, as well as the ancient teachings, informs man regarding the wasteful methods employed by him, and the methods which will obviate these.

Human food material may be divided into three general classes, as follows: (1) Proteid or nitrogenous foods, such as meats, nuts, peas, beans, etc., which are the plastic foods or tissue-builders of the system; (2) the carbohydrates, such as sugars, starches, gums, etc., which are both tissue-builders and heat-producers; (3) the fats, such as animal fats, vegetable oils, butter, etc., which serve principally as heat-producers.

Various authorities have many differing theories regarding the proportions in which the various food-elements should enter into the ordinary diet. But all agree that a variety is needed, and that a well balanced diet consists of articles of food from each class, in about the proportion usually observed in the usual menu of "middle-class" families. The very poor often are unable to obtain many articles of nourishing food, while the very rich often neglect the truly nourishing foods in favor of the "fancy dishes." The average gives us the best selection. A well-known authority was fond of stating that in his opinion the well balanced diet was clearly represented by the sentence: "Bread and butter, beefsteak, potatoes, eggs, and milk," and that variations of the menu would be equally well balanced, providing the same general rule was followed.

It was one of the favorite theories of the ancient occultists that all "sex foods" contain more Vril than other classes of food. By "sex foods" is meant such animal or vegetable products as contain either the reproductive cell or seed, or else serve to nourish the young animal or plant. In the first mentioned class we find eggs, nuts, fruits, grain, corn, berries, which contain the "seed" of reproductive life. In the second class we have milk, cream, butter, the fruit-juices, syrups. The theory was that nature gave in concentrated form the Vril needed by the young growing animal or plant. While modern science has not as yet adopted this idea of the ancient occultists, there are indications that such recognition and approval is not so very far off. The growing popularity of nuts and fruits as articles of diet, the increase of interest in the milk diet, the increasing use of fruit-juices, show that human experience is verifying the ancient theories.

But we are only indirectly concerned with the question of "what kind of food." Our principal concern in this book is rather "*how* food should be eaten." The ancient occultists laid great stress upon the importance of the proper mastication of food, and modern science is becoming very much interested in the subject. In actual practice the old occultists practised many of the fundamental principles that are found in the modern popular theory called "Fletcherism," except that they did not carry the matter to such an extreme as some of the

modern teachers on the subject.  The ancient
teachers held that all food should be thoroughly
masticated until it was reduced to a pulp and
was then almost unconsciously swallowed.
They carried this to such an extent that they
even followed the plan of mastication when a
mouthful of milk was taken, and when the
softest foods were placed in the mouth.  They
did not have the knowledge of the chemistry
of foods possessed by modern science, but their
experience taught them that food masticated
in this way gave the greatest nourishment,
and, what to them was equally important, that
in this way the nerve-ends of the tongue and
mouth absorbed a supply of concentrated Vril
from the food.  They held that the nerves of
the tongue and mouth alone were capable of
performing this office, and that after the food
passed down the throat there was no possibility
of the absorption of Vril from it.

The ancient occultists held that so long as
there remains "taste" in the mouthful of
food, there is Vril to be found in it.  When
the "taste" disappears, the Vril has been absorbed.  Consequently they ate slowly, and
masticated each mouthful carefully so as to extract the greatest amount of "taste" from it.

They claimed that this method of eating not only served to extract the largest amount of Vril from the food, but also gave to the person eating it the fullest epicurean pleasure. They claimed that they obtained a pleasure from eating that the glutton could never experience or even conceive. Accepting this as true, it is further evident, by reason of the physiological principles involved, that food so eaten is thoroughly saturated with saliva and more easily digested by the stomach and intestines when finally swallowed, and that there is consequently but a trifling amount of waste, and a freedom from overloading the stomach. By giving the stomach only an easy task to perform, we are enabled to employ the energy and blood (generally used in the processes of digestion) for service in the brain. The occultists were always "clear in the head," and never suffered the feeling of over-eating and brain-lethargy, neither did they acquire dyspepsia or other disorders of the digestive organism. The student will do well to experiment with this plan of eating, or at least partially adopt it in his everyday life. We promise that if he does this, he will before long experience a new feeling of energy, health, vigor, vitality, and virility, which will prove to him the soundness of the method.

We have no intention of prescribing a dietary for students of this book. Such information must be looked for in works on the subject of nutrition and diet. But in order to answer the very natural questions which frequently arise in this connection, we would say that the ancient occultists, as a rule, lived very simply and followed the rule of " eating to live " rather than "living to eat." Yet such is the law of compensation to be found throughout nature, that they obtained far greater pleasure in their nourishment than did the gourmands and gluttons of their times. This principle is true throughout all nature — avoid excesses and thus experience the true normal satisfaction in all of nature's functionings. He who would seek satisfaction in excess but defeats his object; while he who religiously avoids excess attains that which the extremists miss.

The ancient occultists, while avoiding artificial systems, and while keeping as close to nature as possible, found that their natural instincts (freed from excesses of any kind) inclined them toward a diet of nuts, fruits, milk, eggs, grain, butter, juices, vegetable oils, all of

which, it will be noticed, come under the classi-
fication of "sex foods," as previously mentioned. Even the vegetable oils, such as olive
oil, are found to have some association with
"seeds" or the material surrounding the same.
Milk, butter, and the fruit juices come under
the category of nourishment for the sprouting
seed, or growing young thing. We are of the
opinion that the ancient occultists did not deliberately select this dietary from any specially
preconceived theory, but that, on the contrary,
they found by experiment and experience that
this class of foods served their purposes better
than any other. Of course the very natural
explanation is seen in the fact that nature bends
special energy toward supplying the embryo
with the most nourishing and the most vitally-
powerful material — this being true in both animal and plant life. It is very probable that
this theory will be worked out in detail, in the
light of modern science, by some scientific in-
vestigators in the near future. In the mean-
time, we may do well to take this leaf of experience from the book of life of the ancient
occultists, even in the absence of a detailed
theory.

The ancient occultists also held that water

contains a certain amount of available Vril, which man may extract to advantage by scientific methods of drinking. Accordingly they drank only in small sips, allowing the water to remain in the mouth a few moments before swallowing, during which time it came in continued contact with the nerves of the tongue and mouth. They held that after being swallowed, the water yields no Vril to the body, and serves merely the very useful purpose of the irrigation of the system and the carrying away of refuse material; that no one could ever experience the real pleasure of drinking except in this way. So long as available Vril remains in the water, the tongue and mouth experience a peculiar feeling or sense of satisfaction and gratification, which is unknown to those who *pour* the water down their throats. The increasing use of "straws," or "sippers" by modern persons in drinking lemonade, iced-tea, and other liquids, would seem to indicate that this satisfaction or gratification is becoming known, even though its reason is not suspected. In this way the very *essence* of the water or cooling beverage is absorbed, and the person feels correspondingly refreshed. The plan may be employed to equal advantage in hot drinks, although the ancient occultists re-frained from hot drinks except for the purpose of occasionally "washing out" the stomach and intestines, or of correcting some physical indisposition, the latter, however, being quite rare among them by reason of the life they led.

We trust that in the spirit of investigation and knowledge, at least, the student will experiment with the above indicated methods of eating and drinking, in order to demonstrate to his own satisfaction the advantages of obtaining the Vril contained in food and water. In connection with the methods of breathing which will now be taken up, the aforesaid methods will be found to afford a method of cultivating and preserving physical well-being which will be far ahead of the more complicated systems advised and exploited by the teachers of hygiene and physical culture. The advantage lies in the quick results obtained, as well as in the fact that one does not have to seek for material outside of the everyday things of nature. All that is required is that one manifests his appreciation of nature's bounty in a rational manner. It is merely an intelligent "return to nature."

# LESSON VII

A S we have said in a preceding lesson, Vril
is found in a high degree in the precise
combination required for transmutation into
human vital energy and nervous force, in the
atmospheric air which man constantly breathes
into his lungs.  But science does not admit this
any more than it does the existence of Vril in
food and water.  To science, air is merely a
combination of oxygen and nitrogen with a
mixture of carbureted hydrogen and carbonic
acid, a trace of ammonia, and a suggestion of
the four newly discovered atmospheric elements, *viz.:* argon, crypton, metargon, and
neon — or, more strictly, oxygen and nitrogen
holding a mixture of several other substances
in small proportions.  But the occult teachings
have always held that in the atmospheric air of
the earth there is to be found Vril in a high
degree of potency, and in a condition which
renders it very easily absorbed and assimilated
by the nervous system of plants, animals, and

64

human beings. It would seem that the special combination of oxygen and nitrogen produces a condition in which the element of Vril is easily liberated under certain conditions, in such form as to be easily transmuted and absorbed.

To the physiologist the sole purpose of breathing is that of oxygenating the blood and burning up the waste matter of the system. So important is this function that man is unable to exist for more than a few minutes without fresh air. Without correct habits of breathing, no living creature can hope to live the average lifetime of its kind. So much importance does modern hygiene attach to the subject of correct breathing, that a vigorous attack is being made upon the old-fashioned habit of keeping houses and rooms tightly closed, and a campaign of "open air cure" is under way under the leadership of enthusiastic physicians.

But highly important as is *this* function of breathing, it is no more important than the twin-function attached to it by the Arcane teaching. The latter is the function by means of which the human system absorbs, transmutes, and stores away a supply of Vril from the atmospheric air in the course of ordinary

**breathing.** When it is known that at least eighty-five per cent of the Vril used in the human body is obtained directly from the air, the importance of breathing, in relation to this function, may be appreciated. Not only does the human system obtain Vril directly from the air, but it obtains it indirectly also from the same source. For instance, the Vril in the food has originally been obtained from the air. Also it is known that the inherent charge of Vril in water has been in some way absorbed from the air. Water that has become " stale " may be given new energy by being poured from cup to cup in such a way as to allow it to pass through the air. And it is a matter of common knowledge that distilled water lacks a " something " that can be given it only by passing it through the air in the manner above described, —that " something " is Vril.

The Arcane teaching is not explicit in the direction of explaining the exact physiological process by which the system acquires its supply of Vril from the air in the ordinary process of breathing. All that is said on this score would seem to indicate that the sympathetic nervous system plays an important part in the absorption and transmutation, and that the various

ganglia and plexi of the system act as storage
batteries or reservoirs of Vril, from which the
entire nervous system draws its regular supply,
and its emergency supply in case of unusual
need. Moreover, all the occult teachings insist
that the preliminary absorption of Vril is dependent to some extent upon the passage of air
through the nasal passages and the continua-
tion thereof, and that "mouth-breathing" in
some way fails to produce the same result. It
is thought probable that some of the delicate
nerves which are involved in the sense of smell
may in some way have a secondary part to play
in the preliminary function of the absorption
of Vril.

It is a fact acknowledged by physiologists
that persons who breathe through the mouth
are not nearly so healthy as those who habitually breathe through the nostrils. This fact is
known to the savage races, many of whom take
great care in forcing their infants to acquire
the habit of nostril-breathing and to avoid
mouth-breathing. Children afflicted with ade-
noids (a growth or swelling produced by the
overgrowth of the adenoid tissue in the roof of
the pharynx), which interfere with correct
nasal breathing, are usually deficient in phys-

ical and mental vigor. The slight operation required for the removal of the growth works almost a miracle, the former sufferers manifesting from the start increased physical vitality and mental energy. In many other ways the report of modern physiology agrees with that of the ancient occult teachings regarding the matter of nostril-breathing as compared with mouth-breathing.

Occultists who practice breathing methods for the purpose of the absorption of Vril frequently moisten each nostril before beginning their exercises. This plan is held to increase the power of the nerves of the nasal channel, and to increase the sense of smell as well. Some of the Oriental occultists draw water by suction up through the nasal passages, allowing it to escape through the mouth by means of the canal connecting the nose with the throat. This plan, by the way, is said to be a preventive of nasal disorders such as catarrh. The nostrils should always be kept clear of obstructions, and a healthy condition preserved.

Another fact known to the ancient occultists which also is unknown to modern physiology is that *the individual may largely influence the power of absorption of Vril by the action of*

*the mind, in the form of ideation and use of
will-power* — that is to say, by the familiar
process of visualization or the forming of a
mental picture, backed up by the use of the
will. To those who may be skeptical as to the
effect of the mind over a physical function of
this kind, we would say that in the first place
the absorption of Vril is somewhat different
from the ordinary physiological function, and
in fact may be considered rather as a psycho-
physiological process than a purely physiological one. Vril is not a material substance, but
a form of energy of a very subtle nature, filling
a space in the scale between matter and mind,
and being in a way associated with both.
Therefore it is not unreasonable to suppose
that mind may exercise an effect in its absorption. In the second place, it is a well-known
fact that the mind may and often does have a
very marked effect over the ordinary involuntary processes and organs of the body. The
history of psychic healing establishes this fact,
and moreover it is known that certain men
have developed the power of moving and af-
fecting the involuntary muscles and the sympathetic nervous system by pure acts of will.

It is known that thoughts and mental images

held in the mind of a person may react upon
his physical condition, not only in a general
way but even as regards a particular organ or
part. Thus thoughts and mental pictures of
diseased lungs or liver, or a weak heart, often
result in the manifestation of the exact condition previously pictured in the mind. The
subconscious mind, operating upon the sympathetic nervous system and guided by the harmful auto-suggestion of the person, frequently
adversely affects the organ in question and
impairs its normal functioning. In the same
way the mental picture of a healthy, normal
condition — backed up by a strong will to
manifest such condition — very often results
in the materialization of the ideal. This is the
essence of psychic healing — the very heart of
mental science and of what is called "the new
thought," which is attracting so much attention at this time.

It may be seen that if the mind is capable of
influencing the functions of the body in any
way whatsoever (and there is a mass of testi-
mony regarding the same, which is unques-
tioned and indisputable), there is nothing to
prevent it from influencing the delicate psycho-
physiological functions involved in the absorp-

tion and transmutation of Vril. The gastric juices of the stomach are increased by thoughts and mental pictures of favorite foods; the liver is quickened into activity by good spirits and a happy frame of mind; the reproductive organism is peculiarly affected by the imagination; the saliva flows in response to the thought or memory of some pleasant taste; in short, all the bodily functions seem to be more or less under the influence of the power of the mind, and particularly of the imagination backed up by the will. It is known that the nervous system often gets "in a jangle" by reason of worry and fear. Excessive emotion affects the nerves and often the brain itself. What is there then to seem strange in the idea that the part of the nervous system which is employed in the process of Vril absorption may be encouraged to increased activity by the action of the mind in its phases of ideation and volition? In fact, it would seem very strange if this were not found to be so, when we consider the general principle of the action of mind upon body. When this is understood, we may see the real reason and explanation of much in "psychic phenomena" that has heretofore perplexed us.

## LESSON VIII

### VRIL AND THE BREATH

OCCULTISTS in ancient and modern times have bestowed great attention upon the matter of the influence of the breath upon psychic power and physical well-being. Under various theories they have laid 'down complex rules and announced fantastic methods of breathing for the purpose of increasing one's vitality, physical energy, and psychic power. As is nearly always the case, we find here an example of the bit of truth surrounded by the mass of rubbish — the centre of fact surrounded by the fringe of superstition. Let us consider the matter in the spirit of fairness and understanding, but with the sole purpose of discovering the core of truth and exposing the error with which it is surrounded.

In the first place physiology teaches that correct and normal habits of breathing are necessary to perfect health, and tend to restore health to those who have lost it. It is an elementary truth of physiology that the quality of the blood depends largely upon correct habits of breathing. Unless the blood be properly oxygenated, the waste matter of the system is not properly consumed, the result being that the system is clogged and poisoned by broken down tissue and other debris. Moreover, in such case the cells of the body suffer from the lack of a sufficient amount of oxygen which under normal conditions they receive from the blood. Again, the processes of digestion depend to a certain extent upon the presence of oxygen in the blood, and an absence of oxygen reacts materially upon the digestion and assimilation of food, and consequently upon the welfare of the entire system. Not only this, but the nervous system, also, and even the brain, depend upon the condition of the blood for the nourishment and stimulus which is necessary in their processes. In short, unless the blood be sufficiently oxygenated, the entire system suffers and is unable to function normally and naturally. And, as the oxygenation of the blood is accomplished only by correct habits of breathing, it is seen that the whole system is dependent upon proper breathing. The natural man breathes properly by reason of his habits of life, but the man of our complex and

artificial civilization has lost the natural
method, and few men or women breathe as nature intended they should. So much for the
physiological aspect of the question.

In addition to the physiological side of the
case, as above stated, there is also the side
which ordinary physiology ignores, but which
is of equal importance to the more familiar side
— the phase of breath which is concerned with
the absorption of Vril. We have seen that the
natural man absorbs sufficient Vril in his ordinary breathing, without knowing anything
about the matter — his instinctive mentality
regulates the matter, and co-ordinates the work
of breathing for oxygen and breathing for
Vril, to such a nicety of degree that a perfect
harmony exists, and the observer may fail to
even notice the existence of the dual function
because of the perfect unity thereof. But the
civilized man of the nervous strain and unnatural rush of life in the large cities, not only
does not receive the normal amount of oxygen,
but also fails to absorb the normal amount of
Vril. This is especially deplorable by reason
of the fact that while absorbing much *less* than
the normal amount of Vril, he uses and wastes
much *more* than the normal amount. With

such a man it is indeed a burning of the candle at both ends, and the result is seen in the nervous wrecks and shattered constitutions that are evident on all sides.

It will be seen by the student that before we can consider the special methods of absorbing Vril by breathing, we must first take up the matter of the establishment of natural, normal methods of breathing, which will not only result in one absorbing the normal amount of Vril but will at the same time give him the proper amount of oxygen as indicated by the authorities of physiology. So, in indicating the normal natural process of breathing, we not only aid the student in increasing his Vril supply, but at the same time establish him in habits which must result in an improvement of his general health and state of physical well-being. This is as it should be, for the various phases of the physical being are more or less interdependent, and harmony between them is always desirable.

To many, the idea of instructing the race in correct habits of breathing may seem ridiculous. And so would it be if the race lived normally and naturally. The animal needs no instruction in breathing, neither does the barbarian unspoiled by contact with civilization, the infant born under desirable conditions, or the young child properly reared — at least before it makes the acquaintance of the school-desk. But when it is remembered that physiology informs us that the great majority of civilized persons breathe incorrectly and contrary to nature's evident plan, then we think it may be admitted that instruction along these lines is not unreasonable or unnecessary.

Physiology informs us that there are three general forms of breathing practiced by the race of men, which forms are known by the following names, *viz.:* (1) Clavicular Breathing; (2) Intercostal Breathing; (3) Abdominal Breathing. The distinctive features of each are described as follows:

CLAVICULAR BREATHING. This form of breathing is also termed "collar-bone breathing." It is the form of breathing common to many persons, particularly women, and is considered by the best authorities to be the very worst form of breathing known to the race. It necessitates the expenditure of the greatest amount of effort with the least return — a maximum of energy with a minimum of result. It is held accountable for many diseases of the lungs and throat. Persons practising it habitually, often have harsh, discordant voices. It is found frequently in connection with "mouth-breathing." In this form of breathing the person raises the collar-bone and shoulders, and pulls up the ribs, at the same time drawing in the abdomen. This movement allows only the upper part of the chest to be inflated and only the upper part of the lungs to be filled. But a small quantity of air is admitted to the lungs, as only the upper and smaller portion of the lungs is employed. One may easily convince himself of the folly and inefficacy of this form of breathing, by trying the experiment of raising his shoulders and endeavoring to take a full breath. Then let him drop the shoulders and take a full natural breath, and notice the difference. This experiment is the best possible argument against this injurious method of breathing which is too often habitual with men and women who work over desks, sewing-machines and typewriters.

INTERCOSTAL BREATHING. This form of breathing is also sometimes called "rib breathing." It is a compromise, at the best. While an improvement over clavicular breathing, it is inferior to "abdominal breathing," and far below the standard of the "full breath." In it the upper ribs are inflated, the abdomen drawn in, and the diaphragm pushed upward. It employs the middle part of the chest and lungs, neglecting the lower and upper. It is a favorite method of breathing with many men. Women seldom practise intercostal breathing but pass on to the clavicular breathing mentioned above. It is only a half-way method at the best.

ABDOMINAL BREATHING. This form of breathing is often referred to as "deep breathing," or "diaphragmatic breathing." It has been highly recommended by a number of eminent authorities of late years, and many of the health magazines have made a leading feature of it. Systems and methods of teaching it have been widely advertised, and large prices have been often obtained for a little simple instruction decorated with frills, and dressed up with fancy titles and terms. The principle of abdominal breathing is, however, really quite simple, and its benefits will repay the student who acquaints himself with it and practises it until he has fully mastered it. But we feel that it is but a part of a larger method known as the "full breath," which we shall describe a little further on.

To understand abdominal breathing we must first acquaint ourselves with that wonderful piece of physical mechanism known as the "diaphragm." The diaphragm is defined as: "an inspiratory muscle, and the sole agent in tranquil respiration. It is the muscular septum between the thorax and the adbomen. It assists the abdominal muscles powerfully in expulsion, each act of that kind being accompanied or preceded by a deep inspiration. It also comes into play in hiccough and sobbing, laughing and crying." In simple terms, the diaphragm is a strong plate-shaped muscle which divides the chest and its contents from the abdomen and its contents. At rest, it is arched upward in the centre, like the inside of an inverted bowl, the "sky," or as an arched dome appears to us from below. Viewed from the chest the upper side or surface of the diaphagm would seem like the round top of a man's Derby hat, or the rounded top of a hill. In normal breathing, the diaphragm is flattened out by the arched dome pressing downward. This movement causes the diaphragm to bear downward on the contents of the abdomen,

and the abdomen is pressed outward in front
and at the sides. This movement occurs in abdominal breathing.

In abdominal breathing, the lower part of
the lungs is filled, the diaphragm is pressed
down and the abdomen is pressed out in front
and at the sides, as above described. It is difficult to correctly describe the exact motions
of abdominal breathing, but the student may
acquire the same by practice, using the above
description as a basis. By "bearing down"
on the abdomen by lowering the diaphragm
and pressing out the abdominal muscles, the
lower lungs are given space and free movement, and the deep breath is instinctively inhaled. A little practice will enable anyone to
demonstrate this for himself or herself, much
better than by reading pages of printed instruction.

FULL BREATHING. The best authorities
agree that the best possible form of breathing
is that which *is based on abdominal breathing,
but which also includes the filling of the middle and upper part of the lungs as well.* By
what may seem to be a striking coincidence, it
is noted that this particular form of breathing
is that which was taught by the ancient Arc-

ane teachers to their students as a means of increasing the absorption of Vril. But the coincidence is quite a natural one and it would be indeed strange had it not occurred. For this "full breathing" method is the true, natural, normal method of breathing which natural man instinctively employs. It not only fills every part of the lungs, and exercises every part of the chest — not only secures the greatest possible amount of oxygen and Vril — but also obtains the greatest returns from the least comparative effort. It is an example of the universal economy of nature — just as marked as is the economy of the form of the wax cell of the bee's honeycomb.

In full breathing, all of the respiratory muscles are called into play; the entire area of the lungs is used; the entire machinery of the respiratory organism is exercised, strengthened and developed. There is every evidence that this, and this alone, is nature's normal method of breathing. Moreover, it is known that the hardiest races of men have practiced this form of breathing. We know this from the modern instances, and because the statuary of ancient Greece shows that muscular development of the abdomen and chest which comes only from this form of breathing. It is the first word of nature to man regarding breathing — it is the last word of science to man on the same subject. It is the best natural method — it is the best scientific method.

Full breathing is not an artificial system or method of breathing but is rather a return to natural normal methods and habits. But, nevertheless, it will require some practice on the part of many students hereof, by reason of the fact that they have lost their natural instinct in the matter, and are under the dominion of the "second nature" of false habit. Before the instinctive habit may be resumed, the effect of the false habit must be overcome, and this usually takes time. The best, and indeed almost the only way of counteracting and defeating any objectionable habit, is to practice its opposite — and this rule applies here with great force. The only way to get rid of the old habit is to practise the new. And the only way to acquire the new is to practice it. So, from both angles, the importance of practice is seen.

EXERCISE: The following exercise will serve to develop the full breath, if conscientiously practised.

(1) Standing erect, or sitting in a natural
position, inhale slowly through the nostrils,
and according to the method of "abdominal
breathing" fill the lower lungs, press down the
diaphragm, and push out the abdomen in front
and at the sides; then in a continuous effort
(2) fill the middle part of the chest and lungs,
as in intercostal breathing, pressing outward
the mid-ribs, breast-bone and chest; then in
the same continuous effort (3) fill the upper
portion of the lungs, as in clavicular breathing, lifting the upper portion of the chest,
slightly raising the collar-bone, slightly drawing in the abdomen and thus raising the diaphragm, as heretofore explained.

It will be noticed that this method of "full
breathing" is really a combination of the three
forms of breathing previously described, beginning with the abdominal, proceeding to the
intercostal, and finishing with the clavicular
method.   But the student is cautioned against
proceeding as if there were three distinct and
separated stages of the process.  *There is but
one continuous process,* rising gradually from
the lower part of the lungs to the middle portion, and then to the upper portion.   A uni-
form continuous muscular movement is ef-

fected, the several regions being called into action in a rising sequence. *All disconnected, spasmodic, jerky motion should be avoided.* A little practice will result in the acquirement of the continuous inhalation.

The inhaled air should be retained for a moment, and then exhaled naturally and easily. No attempt should be made to unduly *retain* the breath, as is taught by some schools of breathing. There is nothing to be gained by the retention in the lungs of stale, exhausted air; besides which, there is always more or less of *strain* in this forced retention, as the whole process is unnatural. In natural normal breathing there is no sense of strain or effort, when once the habit is acquired, or rather re-acquired. The infant or young child manifests no effort or strain in breathing, and neither should the adult.

Some teachers announce a variety of methods of breathing, which upon examination are found for the most part to consist of fantastic and fanciful processes, designed evidently to impress the student with the novelty, and presumably great virtue, of these newly invented methods.   There is only one safe and sane rule, and that is to *go back to nature*. The " full breath " is nature's own method. If you doubt this, watch the motions of a sleeping, healthy child, or sturdy infant.

# LESSON IX

I N many treatises upon psychic breathing, or
other occult teachings in which the breath
is employed in the process of the absorption of
Vril (under some one of the names applied to
it), we find many fanciful methods of breathing given, great stress being laid upon the supposed merits of each. A little close analysis will
show that these methods are divided into two
classes, *viz.:* (1) methods in which the breath
is inhaled, retained, and exhaled, in some fanciful manner — often according to the count of
so many moments to each step in the process,
or else in some fantastic accompaniment. Another variation of this class of methods is
that of inhaling through one nostril, exhaling
through the other, and then reversing the order of nostrils. The best authorities hold that
there is no virtue whatsoever in the fanciful
form of these methods, outside of the sugges-
tive effect upon the imagination of the person, the auto-suggestion causing some benefit

by reason of the belief of the person setting into effect the activities of the subconscious mind, and accordingly of the physical organs by means of the sympathetic nervous system. These methods are but variations of the principle underlying "faith healing," and their results are obtained in the same way. (2) The second class of these fanciful methods consists simply of combinations of well-known physical-culture movements, with an emphasis laid upon the use of the breath in their performance. These exercises, of course, have their value in the direction of promoting physical culture, the breathing phase being merely incidental and secondary.

It will be seen that the above explained fanciful methods, while possessing no special value in themselves, nevertheless may result in good, if practiced in moderation and if excess is avoided. There are some exercises given, however, which we feel lay undue emphasis upon the retained breath, and upon the length of time employed in inhaling and exhaling. In our opinion there is a possibility of a strain in such practices, and we do not recommend them, particularly when it is remembered that they have no real physiological or psychical value.

We have heard of teachers of some of these systems teaching classes of persons to inhale very slowly, and to retain the breath until a feeling of giddiness arose, the peculiar " swimmy " feeling thus experienced being held to be proof of the development of some high psychic state.    The slightest acquaintance with elementary physiology, however, should teach one that the dizziness is not a psychic state, but arises from the poisoning of the body by the carbonic acid gas generated in the system, which under natural conditions would have been expelled, and also from the fact that the body and brain are crying out " Oxygen! send us oxygen, or we perish!"    In short, instead of a state of psychic power being attained, there is really a state of partial asphyxiation induced.

The Arcane teachers do not teach any of the above mentioned fantastic or fanciful methods. On the contrary, they hold that there is no better way of absorbing Vril, under ordinary circumstances, than the " full breathing " method of nature.    They hold that the man or woman who acquires or re-acquires the habit of proper natural " full breathing " will usually absorb a normal degree of Vril.    But they hold also that an additional amount of Vril is often needed by those living under conditions which tend to deplete them of their Vril by excessive use or excessive waste. They accordingly teach methods by which additional Vril may be absorbed according to the desire or need of the person. But this method of absorption does not consist of any fanciful physical method or exercise, but *depends upon the use of the mind* in connection with the natural normal process of breathing. The Arcane method is psycho-physical, rather than physical. Those of our students who have studied the previous works of this series will understand the power and effect of the mind upon the physical functions, without our going into the matter in detail in this place.

The secret of the Arcane method of Vril absorption consists of the fact that *the nervous system may be spurred to redoubled efficiency by the action of the mind directed upon it*. In Lesson X of " The Arcane Formulas, or Mental Alchemy," which lesson is entitled " Mentalism in a Nutshell," is explained the method of psychic " visualization " or the forming and holding of the mental image of things and conditions which one wishes to realize objectively

and in material form. In the same lesson is
explained the use of the will in the materialization and objectification of desired conditions.
On page 97 of the said book and lesson,
you will find the following paragraph:
*" The secret of mental alchemy may be stated
as consisting first, last and always, of the art
of mental imaging, reinforced by the will.   .   .*
While to the beginner the subject of mentalism
may seem a very complicated one, the advanced occultist knows it to be the very extreme of simplicity. *Mental alchemy, under
whatever name it may masquerade, may be
found to consist, at the last, of simply the
power to create strong, clear, mental images,
and to project them into the outer world by
means of the concentrated will.   .   .* You
will find that all you have ever read on the subject may be 'boiled down' to the above stated
principle.   The rest is a mere matter of detail.   This single statement is 'mentalism in a
nutshell.' "

We have quoted from the earlier work of
this series in order to emphasize the fact that
the power of psychic visualization, backed by
the power of the will, is the secret of Vril absorption, as it is of all psychic or psycho-

physical phenomena. The first step in Vril absorption is the realization by the student that there exists in the atmospheric air a universal supply of Vril in such phase and condition as to render it easily assimilated by the nervous system of man and other living creatures. The second step is the formation of *a clear mental picture* of this universal supply of Vril. Of course, Vril having no definite shape or form, color or outward appearance, the mind cannot form a picture of it as a thing of form, color or other tangible attribute. But the mind *can image* it, as it would *image* a space filled with electrical power, magnetism, or ether. The mind must enter into a consciousness of the *presence* of Vril in space, all around one, and in every atom of air that is breathed. This *consciousness of that presence* must be gained before further progress is possible — it must be dwelt upon mentally until the mind grasps its reality and becomes conscious of its presence, just as one is conscious of the presence of space itself. In the degree that this consciousness is gained, so is the degree of manifestation possible.

The next step is the realization and mental imaging of the faculty of the nervous system to absorb such amount of Vril as is required, in response to the mandate of the will. The mind must visualize the nerves as absorbing the Vril from the air, just as it can visualize the lungs absorbing oxygen from the same source. The one must be seen to be as real as the other. Of course the nerves will absorb Vril in the ordinary way whether or not one is conscious of the process — in fact, this is the way that the average person absorbs Vril — but in order to *increase* the absorptive power of the system, the mind must be employed in the manner above described. This process imparts to the absorptive function an increased efficiency, just as thought-force is known to increase the efficiency of the stomach, liver or other organs of the body.

The final step is the use of the will in the direction of *commanding* the system to absorb a greater amount of Vril. After the reason recognizes the possibility of this process, and the imagination pictures it as being performed, then the will may be directed to the task of demanding its performance. To those to whom this may seem a strange statement, we would say that the majority of our physical actions are evolved in just this way. With the

exception of a few elementary instinctive actions which are performed almost automatically, the young animal, and particularly the
young human child, first realizes that a movement may be made, then sees it being made by
the imaginative or ideative faculties, and then
deliberately *wills* it to be made. The child
follows this process in learning to use its legs
in walking; in using its hands in taking hold
of a thing and guiding it to its mouth; and
afterward in directing its hand to write, use
the knife and fork or perform similar offices.
The story of evolution as told by Lamarck and
his school tells us that the life-forms have
gradually developed new functions in this way,
the physical organ evolving in response to the
mental picture and desire. In forming the
mental picture until it becomes firmly fixed in
the subconscious mind, and then reinforcing
and enforcing it by the will, the "nature" of
the person develops the faculty of increased
power of absorption of Vril, which is manifested in response to the will of the person.

VRIL-ABSORPTION EXERCISE. The following exercise will serve as a general guide to
those who wish to increase their power of Vril
absorption. (1) Practise the "full breath"

(as heretofore described), and, *while inhaling, picture in your mind the absorption of Vril first by the nerves of the nasal cavity and the back of the head, and then by the cells of the lungs, at the same time " willing " that the Vril be so absorbed.* Or, if it is preferred, it may be stated in this manner: *WILL that the system absorb an increased amount of Vril, and at the same mentally picture the process of absorption.* Or perhaps a third form will be easier for some: *WILL the Vril absorption, and at the same time " feel " that it is under way.*

After a little practice the student will find that the system will become as responsive to the will in this function, as the lungs are responsive to the will when one decides to take a breath fuller and deeper than usual. And, in the same way, the person will become almost as vividly *conscious* of the influx of Vril as he is of the influx of air in breathing. A little practice will demonstrate this to the student of his own actual experience, much better than can we in pages of written description and statement. Imagine what it would be to attempt to describe the sensation of breathing to a creature that had never breathed — a visitor for instance, from some distant star where breathing was unknown. Or imagine describing the sensation of seeing the color "scarlet," to a man born blind. Or the sensation of the taste of sugar, to one who had never tasted anything sweet. Sensations of this kind must be experienced in order to be understood. The student has the matter in his own hands —his experience and actual knowledge depend upon his own practice.

It is not intended that one shall practise this conscious Vril absorption all the time — this is not necessary. Moreover, it is not practicable, for the process requires the concentration of attention upon the task, and one requires the attention for other purposes. It is sufficient for one to practise this method only when he feels that his Vril supply is depleted, or just before engaging in work that will probably require additional energy. One may absorb additional Vril while engaged in other work, without disturbing his occupation — it requires but a moment or two — just as the flying locomotive takes up water without stopping. It will be found to be an excellent plan to practise some light physical-culture exercise in the morning before arising, and then to devote a few moments to Vril absorption. This will start one well in the work of the day. When fatigued during the day, a moment's relaxation and practice of Vril absorption will yield great benefit. There are no set rules to be observed in this matter. Each one must use his own judgment, and fit the method to his own inclination and necessities. *Absorb Vril whenever you feel you need it.*

# LESSON X

W HEN the student has acquired the knack of Vril absorption, he may apply the power of Vril to his physical requirements in many ways. He will have laid up a reserve store of Vril in the solar plexus and other centres, which he may direct and distribute to the various parts and organs of his body, at will. It is possible for anyone, with a little practice, to acquire the art of directing the flow of Vril to any particular part of the body. This will be found very advantageous in the treatment of physical troubles and weaknesses. When any part of the body is found to lack proper vitality, or when any organ shows signs of imperfect functioning, a supply of Vril directed to that part or organ will be found to be highly beneficial in the direction of vitalizing and stimulating the part or organ in question. This is true not only of organs like the stomach or liver, but also of the great nerve centres of the body, including the spinal cord and even the brain itself. Treatment of the spinal cord in this way will result in imparting a new spirit of vitality and energy to the entire system, and is one of the best tonic treatments known to psycho-physiology. The following general directions will serve to give the student the key to the many forms of application possible under it. The general principle once clearly understood and firmly grasped, the student may apply it as indicated by his own particular requirements and necessities, and in such manner as seems preferable to him.

GENERAL DIRECTIONS. Either sit in a comfortable position, or else recline in an easy position, relaxing every muscle and quieting every nerve. Then concentrate the attention upon the solar plexus (or the region of the pit of the stomach just where the ribs spread apart), and awaken your consciousness of the storage of a reserve supply of Vril at this point. Then *will* that some of this Vril supply shall flow along the nerves to whatever part of the body you wish to energize. If the part to be energized is situated *above* the solar plexus, you must mentally and by an effort of the will, *draw upward* the Vril current; if the part to be energized is situated *below* the solar plexus, you must in the same way mentally *push downward* the current. In either case you must accompany the will effort by the mental picture and consciousness of the actual passage of the current. It may take you a little time to acquire the peculiar "knack" of directing the current in this way, but after a little practice you will find it very easy, in fact it will become almost "second nature" to you to send the current whenever you recognize the need of it.

When you feel generally tired, exhausted, or "used up," it will be found beneficial to treat the whole body in this way. In special cases, particular parts or organs may be so treated. A feeling of relief will be experienced in the part treated, in a few moments. In case of headaches, or other *pains*, relief may often be obtained by first *flushing* the affected part with Vril (in the manner above described), and then reversing the process and drawing away the current — this plan tending to equalize the circulation and the nerve currents, and thus to restore normal conditions. Cold feet often may be relieved by stimulating them with a supply of Vril. Stiff muscles or rheumatic joints often are relieved in this way. In fact, one who can so direct and distribute the Vril currents is practical master of his or her own body, and may successfully "treat" himself or herself in this way to great advantage. The brain may be stimulated by sending it a strong current of Vril, or it may be rested by first "flushing" it with Vril and then drawing away the supply and allowing the brain to rest quietly in a relaxed condition of peace and comfort.

GENERAL SELF-TREATMENT. A form of general self-treatment by Vril currents, in the direction of a general vitalization and energization of the entire system, is herewith suggested: (1) Lie in a comfortable position, and concentrate the attention upon the solar plexus, awakening a consciousness of the presence there of the reserve-supply of Vril. Then direct the current downward to the feet — first to the left foot and then to the right — until you can feel the energy manifesting in them. In some cases a slight tingling may be felt, while in others merely a general "feeling" or subconscious "awareness" is manifest. Then treat the lower part of the legs in the same order; then the thighs; then the reproductive region; then the abdomen and the lower internal organs; then stimulate the solar plexus itself; then the lungs and throat. After having treated the various organs and parts of the body in this manner, reverse the current and cause it to flow down the spinal column, sweeping it repeatedly from top to bottom, allowing some of the current to flow out through the connected nerves. Next concentrate the attention upon the sacral plexus, at the lower part of the spine — giving to this region a decided stimulation. Finally, direct the Vril to the nerves and muscles of the neck, and then to the brain, giving the latter a good "flushing," and then withdrawing the current by a reverse impulse and direction of the will. Rest quietly a few moments, and you will arise refreshed and energized. Variations may be applied to this general treatment, but the general order above suggested will be found to be adapted to the majority of cases.

SPECIAL SELF-TREATMENT: In cases of local pain or physical disorder, one may treat himself not only in the above stated general manner, but also by specially concentrated currents of Vril directed by the use of the hands. In this case the Vril flows down the nerves of the arm and hands and into the affected parts with renewed and increased force and effect. Passing the hands over the affected parts, or holding them there, at the same time *willing* that a steady, continuous, and powerful flow of Vril pass through them and into the part, will be found quite effective in many instances. If preferred, the Vril may be forced into the part in this manner by a series of mental "pushes" or "pumping motions." Some prefer one plan, and some the other. Both should be tried, and the one best adapted to the particular wants of the person adopted and applied thereafter.

TREATMENT OF OTHER PERSONS: The student may treat other persons in the same way as indicated in the above directions for self-treatment. The principle is the same in all cases. The knowledge of the direction and distribution of Vril to the bodies of other persons constitutes the secret of what is popularly known as "magnetic healing." There is no special new principle involved in the treatment of others. Treat the other person just as you would treat a part of your own body. The current of Vril will flow into the affected part of the other person and back to yourself. Always place *both* hands on the other person during the treatment, in order to complete the connection in this way. After the treatment, it will be well for the healer to treat himself briefly, and to recharge himself with Vril by the method previously described. In this way he will never suffer from depletion of Vril, and will avoid "taking on the condition" of the patient which often occurs to psychic healers who are not acquainted with the means of recuperating and protecting themselves.

Interesting experiments have been tried along the lines of charging water with Vril, by holding the glass in one's hands and sending the current into it. Some magnetic healers have made quite a feature of charging water in this way, and then giving it to their patients to drink in sips, in addition to the regular treatment. We mention it here merely as a matter of general interest, and as a suggestion for experiment on the part of our students. We feel that, interesting though it may be, it is not a necessary or important part of treatment by Vril, for the reason that the course above outlined should be sufficiently successful without the assistance of such methods.

By reason of the simplicity of the methods suggested and the absence of all attempts to dress the subject in fanciful and mystic verbal garb and imagery, there is danger of the average student failing to appreciate the benefits that may be gained by the use of Vril in the manner indicated in this lesson, and of his failing to realize the importance of the information herein given. We warn the student against undervaluing any knowledge or instruction merely because it may be stated simply and plainly. It is no easy matter to reduce teaching of this kind to simple plain terms, and equally simple methods, for this task is really the condensation into a few lines of the experience of many years and of many persons. It is much easier to elaborate the matter in detailed technical style, than to reduce it to terms and methods capable of being understood and applied by all persons of average intelligence. The student must not forget that behind this simple exposition and explanation, and the equally simple methods of application, there is to be found one of the greatest and most wonderful of nature's forces, the real inner meaning of which will probably never be fully known to the mind of man. The final secret is bound up with the secret of Life itself. The student who masters these instructions and methods is brought in touch with this great force of Life, and is enabled to apply its energies at will. Let him beware of undervaluing the power he is using, simply because it is capable of simple, plain application. And let him beware, further, of allowing familiarity with this power to develop into contempt of it. Nature does not approve of belittling or trifling with her great forces. Triflers who enter the field of psychism or occultism frequently are brought to a rather vigorous realization of the fact that they are but pygmies playing with titanic forces. On the other hand, there is something in nature which seems to approve of the right use of its mighty forces, and which encourages and aids those who employ these forces in the proper spirit and toward worthy ends. And the right use of vital-energy, life-force, Vril, is always in the direction of LIFE and HEALTH.

## LESSON XI

THE Arcane teachings hold that not only does the wise person store up a sufficient supply of Vril to meet sudden and unexpected demands — not only does he direct and distribute Vril to meet the requirements of his physical and mental system — but he also avoids unnecessary waste and dissipation of Vril power, and strives to stop all leaks of energy. Such person practices not only industry and thrift in relation to Vril, but also manifests a wise economy regarding its conservation.

Vril waste and dissipation occurs in two ways, *viz.:* (1) emotional waste; and (2) physical waste. The majority of persons are more or less prodigals along one or both of the above stated lines. They turn on the emotional or physical faucet, and allow Vril to drip and dribble almost constantly — pure waste.

Emotional waste is habitual with many persons who fail to realize that in every useless flow of emotional activity they are really dis-

sipating a portion of the life-power and vital
energy. Not only does this emotional dissipation result in a drain on the life energies, but,
like any other form of dissipation, it results
also in killing the healthy and normal emotional expression, replacing the latter with a
false emotional activity which is without real
feeling and which seeks constant excitement
and stimulus as the drunkard seeks drink, and
the drug habituate his particular narcotic or
stimulant.

One may avoid this emotional waste by
watching carefully the formation of emotional
habits. As an authority says: " All emotions
deepen by repetition. If one allows an unde-
sirable feeling to master him once, he should
be on the watch to check that feeling at the
start on the occasion of the second manifestation. The man who falls into a rage once, falls
into the same emotion easier a second time; the
man who keeps cool once under trying circumstances, will be more easily able to control himself the next time.  .  . The truth cannot be
too strongly emphasized, that a habit of emotional feeling is, at the outset, often the result
of an intellectual habit. Summon different
ideas to the mind, and notice how the emotion

changes with the idea. . . to repress certain
trains of feeling, repress the ideas that give
them birth. This will have restraining power,
even when the emotional state tends to bring up
a consonant idea, just as a fire may suggest put-
ting fuel on it."

Emotional waste may also be prevented by
carefully training oneself to control the physical expression usually accompanying the
feeling or emotion. An authority says: "By
restraining the expression of an emotion, we
can frequently throttle it; by inducing an
expression, we can often cause its allied emotion. . . We know that animals, barbarians,
and children generally allow motor discharges
without inhibition, and that control comes in
some way or other with culture." Another eminent authority says: "Even if we cannot
prevent a feeling from arising, we may possibly
prevent it from spreading, by inhibiting the
organic movement which accompanies it, and
indulgence in which augments it."

An authority says: "Novices frequently
make the mistake of thinking that intense expression of emotion indicates not only a character rich in feeling, but also one that will make
great unselfish sacrifices for the welfare of

others. The truth lies generally in the opposite direction. Many persons expend all their energies in the expression of emotion and have none left for action. Some demonstrative people find it difficult to understand that to feel intense sympathy is not the same as to exert themselves in actually relieving distress. The world could very well spare a million of those who only *feel* for a dozen of those who *act*."

In the volume of this series entitled "The Arcane Formulas," we have devoted considerable space to instruction along the lines of mastering and controlling the emotional nature, not in the direction of killing out or destroying that part of one's mental and spiritual being, but rather in the direction of attaining perfect mastery and control thereof. We have therein instructed the student in the art of "mastering the opposites" of feeling and emotion, that he may secure and maintain the true mental, moral, and spiritual balance and poise. We have said therein: "Acquire the mental 'knack' of rising above the plane of emotional feeling, on to the plane of will, and there calmly watch and observe the storm of emotion without being influenced by it. This is like one sailing in a balloon above the storm clouds which are thundering and flashing lightning beneath him. On the plane of will there is peace and power undreamt of by those still on the emotional plane. . . Never allow yourself to become enmeshed and involved in the emotional storms or activities. Handle the emotions as the master does an instrument — but never yield yourself to the power and influence of slave or instrument, any more than you would yield yourself to the power and influence of some entity outside of yourself."

The study of the Arcane teachings, in the preceding volumes of the series, will do much for anyone who has found himself or herself carried away by emotional storms, or cyclones of feeling, which result in Vril dissipation and waste. The principles therein taught, and the methods therein stated, will do much to impart balance and poise, self-control and self-mastery to those who seek "poise and power." Emotion and feeling play an important part in our lives, and when properly employed are good for us to use — but, even when normally good, they become bad when we allow them to *use us* to the extent that we become subject to them and under their control. Even "the divine gift of sympathy" may become a veritable curse in this way, and may tend to wreck the mental and physical well-being of a person, without in the least benefiting the objects which aroused it originally. We must be strong ourselves before we may help others. As in everything else in life, so in this case we must avoid the extremes or "opposites," and preserve the happy mean in the centre, where alone is poise, power and balance to be found.

Passing from the consideration of this first form of emotional waste of Vril-power, we perceive that the average person manifests an equally harmful waste in his physical life. Waste motion, waste nervous strain, excessive nervous tension, and excessive purposeless physical motion is seen on all sides. The majority of persons are in a state of unrelaxed nervous and muscular tension during their waking hours. Their nerves are tense, and the muscles contracted, without any real cause. Their fingers are beating the "devil's tattoo," and they waste nervous energy to no purpose whatsoever. They whittle pencils, chew toothpicks, or masticate chewing-gum. They do not know the meaning of the word *relaxation,* and have no conception of its physical expression. When talking, these persons throw into the

task sufficient energy to sustain a vigorous ora-
tor through the strain of his greatest effort.
When walking, they expend enough energy to
carry a giant up a steep hill. When riding they
sit on the edge of the car seat, leaning forward
as if they imagined that they were using their
energy to help propel the train to their des-
tination. Poise is unknown to these people who
are burning their Vril candle at both ends.

Such persons should take an object lesson
from a young resting infant, or from a cat in
a relaxed position. The child "lets go" to
perfection. The cat relaxes every muscle and
nerve, and yet so finely organized is it that in
the twinkling of an eye when necessity for possible action arises, its muscles become as steel,
and its nerves as hair-triggers. The cat crouch-
ing before a mouse-hole gives one of nature's
best object lessons in the quality of "relaxed
power." Here we find the latent hair-trigger
nerves, and the potential steel muscles, in a
state of perfection.

The only way to relax properly is to with-
draw the Vril tension from the muscles. And
this is not so easy for those who have contracted the unnatural habits of unnecessary tension. They must first learn how to "let go."

The student wishing to learn how to relax should begin by practicing with the hands, first taking away all tension, and then swinging the hands from the wrists, until they become perfectly limp. Then practise "limbering up" the fingers. Then swing the arms to and fro in the same manner. Then, tense the upper arm and swing the fore-arms freely from the elbow. Then follow the same general course with the legs, until you have them thoroughly "loosened up." Then swing the head about, the neck being made limp. And, finally, lying down, manage to take every bit of Vril-force from the muscles of the whole body, imitating the attitude, position and general condition of the tired baby who has dropped to sleep over its play.

A variation of the "loosening up" exercises may be found in the imitation of a Newfoundland dog shaking himself vigorously — this will give you a good general "limbering up." "Stretching" the limbs, in the familiar motion of the lazy boy, will also be found to give relaxation and rest, and to relieve tension. Conclude the relaxation exercises with the "Bracing-up exercise" given below, which will also be found excellent in case of the tired feeling caused by sitting or standing in one position, or when the brain feels fagged and tired, or when from any mental or physical cause one may feel "stale" and "not fit."

BRACING-UP EXERCISE. Stand erect, and take several natural, easy, "full breaths," combining with them the mental exercise of Vril absorption. Then, holding your arms out in front of you, clench your fists and draw them slowly toward your breast, gradually increasing the muscular tension. Then push your fists out and draw them in (muscles still tensed) several times. Then drop your fists to your sides, and gradually draw them straight up as far as they will go, tensing the muscles as the fists ascend. Repeat several times. Then moving your arms about (with clenched fists) alternately tense and relax the muscles. A few moments of this exercise will fill the upper part of the body with fresh Vril, and will impart a wonderful feeling of energy and power. Similar exercises, employing the legs in alternate tension and relaxation, will likewise vitalize and energize the body below the waist. There are no set motions in this exercise, the whole principle being that of alternate tension and relaxation. The benefits of this exercise, or any similar light exercise,

will be doubled it one will throw his mind into
it.   Picture the benefit to be derived from it,
and while performing the exercise, endeavor to
enter into the consciousness of the action of
Vril, and you will find that the action of the
mind will serve to give to Vril a mighty force
and impulse in the direction or the exercised
parts and their vicinity.

In the field of emotional Vril waste, we find
that the emotional states of anger, hate, jeal-
ousy, fear, worry, and over-anxiety, and the
attempt to vicariously live out the life of another for him or her, are the ones which produce the greatest strain, tension, waste and dissipation.   Steady, calm mental work seldom
wrecks one, while the above emotional states,
and others, expressed to too great a degree,
slowly but surely undermine the nervous system, and react upon mind and body.   In the
same way steady, normal physical exercise or
work seldom affects one injuriously, while the
unnatural nervous and muscular tension before
mentioned, and the nervous physical actions
resulting from the presence of the injurious
emotions to which we have alluded, frequently
strain the physical nature to the utmost.   And,
as in the majority of cases the emotional waste

is manifested in connection with the physical waste,—each serving to feed the other by action and reaction—we may readily see that in Vril waste and dissipation we have the secret of that curse of the age known as neurasthenia or nervous prostration. This is not the result of overwork, as is generally supposed, but is the result of over-worry, undue tension, and lack of mental balance and poise, which serve to waste the life-forces, the vital energies, or Vril. To overcome this trouble it is first necessary to recognize its cause, and then to counteract the cause by following the course directly opposed to it. We trust that in this book we have explained the former, and pointed the way toward the latter.

# LESSON XII

## THE PSYCHIC PHASE OF VRIL

IT is not our purpose to enter into a detailed discussion of mental science, psychic phenomena, or occultism, in this book. In the preceding books of this series we have dwelt upon this subject in some detail, and we must refer thereto the student who is specially interested in this particular field of the teaching. But our consideration of the subject of Vril would be incomplete did we not at least call attention to the part played by Vril in the phenomena generally classed as "psychic," "mental science," or "occult." Therefore we shall in this lesson point out in a general way the office and function of Vril in such phenomena.

PSYCHIC INFLUENCE. In the various phases of what is known as "psychic influence," or the effect of the mind of one person over that of another, Vril plays an important part. In the degree that the thought projections, thought-waves, thought-vibrations (or whatever term may be used), are charged with Vril, so is their effect upon the person receiving them. Just as the degree of clearness in the sound of the telephone depends materially upon the strength of the current operating the system, so does the strength of the Vril current materially determine the power of the thought vibrations sent from one person to another, over a short or long distance. In fact, Vril is the real *force* or *energy* in all manifestations of thought-force — the mind merely serving to project that force by the will, and to color it by the idea or feeling held in the mind. The thought sent forth is colored and charged with Vril by the strength of the feeling or desire manifested, in the majority of cases. But the trained mental scientist or occulist uses his direct will-power to accomplish the same result, using precisely the same method that he does in directing and distributing the Vril to parts of his own body, or to the body of another person when he is giving personal psychic treatments as described in preceding lessons. This fact, understood in connection with what we have said on the subject in the other books of the series above mentioned, gives one the complete key to psychic influence, mental science treatments, and other occult phenomena in which mind acts upon

mind or body over a distance. The general principle is the same in all of these cases. Persons
may be " treated " by sending them thoughts of
strength and vitality, or of courage and success, charged with strong currents of Vril im-
pelled by the will of the sender. In the same
way, one may send to another direct currents
of Vril, and thus increase his or her vitality,
energy, force, and power. Telepathic messages may be increased in power by charging
them with an increased supply of Vril.
Thought-forms sent forth in the manner familiar to occultists, may be energized and vital-
ized by charging them with the dynamic force
of Vril. The student who is interested in this
phase of the matter should study carefully the
lesson " Mentalism in a Nutshell," in the book
of this series entitled " The Arcane Formulas."

SELF-PROTECTION. In the same way the
self-protection by thought-auras, psychic armor, etc., familiar to all occultists may be won-
derfully increased by charging the protective
thought-force with a strong current of Vril.
The ideative power of the mind, and the will,
are used in this process. By forming a strong
mental image of the presence of the protective
thought-aura surrounding the body, and which

is rendered dynamic by currents of Vril, the occultist may surround himself with an armor of protection that will defy all attacks on the part of others. In the same way, one may use Vril in connection with the thought-atmosphere with which he surrounds himself, and which gives the keynote to the attitude of other persons toward him. He may create this mental atmosphere by the character of the thoughts held by him, his mental attitude, or his affirmations, according to the system followed by him — and in either case he may greatly increase the power of this mental atmosphere by charging it with Vril according to the general method which we have repeatedly mentioned in this book — visualization and will-power. This is the explanation of that peculiar "force" or "power" which we feel emanating or flowing from the presence of strong individuals — a force or power which strikes us with almost a physical impact.

As we have already said, we do not purpose entering into a detailed consideration of psychic phenomena in this book. In the above mention of Vril in this connection we have given in a few words, and in simple form, an occult secret which should prove very valuable to all occultists who are not already acquainted with it and who have been contenting themselves by merely using *thought* in their psychic experiments or work. It will be found that this use of Vril will prove to be the missing keystone which is essential to give to the whole psychic arch that strength, unity, and power which it needs. The student will find that it may be added or adapted to any of the many systems of occult practice with which students of the subject may be familiar. It is an "attachment" which may be used in connection with any or all the systems, old or new, ancient or modern.

In this matter, as in a number of others in this book, we have given you the spirit of a great occult method or system in a few plain words. We have condensed it, and given you the essence. We have stated the whole thing in a nutshell. Once more we warn you not to overlook the value and importance of the thing by reason of its simplicity and plainness.

### FINAL ADVICE

You have now read this book through in a more or less hasty way. You have seen some things which have attracted you, and which you have decided to apply in your own life and

work. But you have missed many other things
of equal or perhaps greater value. Therefore,
we ask that you lay this book aside for a few
days, and mentally assimilate that which you
have learned from it. Then take it up again,
and *carefully* re-read and re-study it from beginning to end. Much to your surprise you
will find that there are many things in it which
you have entirely overlooked. Also, that many
things will appear to you in a new light and
with an added meaning. A week or so later,
read and study it for the third time, and you
will have a like result. You will not begin to
understand the real value of the principles announced in this book in less than the three read-
ings above advised. In this connection you
should re-read and re-study the other books of
the series, and each will serve to throw light on
the others. The Arcane Teaching is based upon
certain general principles which are immanent
in every branch and in every phase of it. Each
phase blends into the others. Thus does the
teaching present a unity and a harmony when
each phase is studied and considered in relation to the others.

In conclusion let us use words once before
used in this series: "Oh, Neophyte, in the

Centre of Life shalt thou indeed find poise and power. In the Heart of the Storm shalt thou find peace. He who finds the centre of himself, finds the centre of the Cosmos. For at last they are ONE!"

**FINIS**